ISBN 978-0-483-03417-4
PIBN 10185773

THE PEACE WE NEED.

BY

HENRY A. BOARDMAN, D. D.

THE PEACE WE NEED,

AND HOW TO SECURE IT.

A SERMON

PREACHED IN THE TENTH PRESBYTERIAN CHURCH, PHILADELPHIA, ON THE DAY OF NATIONAL HUMILIATION, JUNE 1, 1865.

BY

HENRY A. BOARDMAN, D. D.

PHILADELPHIA:
JAMES S. CLAXTON,
SUCCESSOR TO WILLIAM S. & ALFRED MARTIEN,
No. 606 CHESTNUT STREET.
1865.

PHILADELPHIA, June 2, 1865.

To the Rev. Henry A. Boardman, D. D., Pastor Tenth Presbyterian Church.

Rev. and Dear Sir—Feeling assured that much good would result from a dissemination of the sentiments contained in your sermon delivered June 1st, the day set apart as one of "Humiliation and Prayer" by the President, we respectfully request that you furnish a copy for publication.

Truly your friends,

ISAAC R. SMITH,
JAMES THOMPSON,
THOMAS A SCOTT,
D. HAYES AGNEW,
JOHN STEWART,
E. P. BORDEN,
A. LOUDON SNOWDEN,
J. B ROSS,
JOHN DICKSON,
JAMES SCHOTT,
BENJ. MARSHALL,
J. SHIPLEY NEWLIN,
H. W. PITKIN.

PHILADELPHIA, June 5, 1865.

Gentlemen—My sermon of Thursday, was the proper and *promised* sequel to that on the "*Peace-Makers*," published a week or two ago. It gratifies me to know that you think the sentiments of the discourse suited to the present crisis; and I cheerfully commit the manuscript to your disposal.

I am, very sincerely, your friend and Pastor,

HENRY A. BOARDMAN.

To ISAAC R SMITH, Esq ,
Hon. JAMES THOMPSON, and others.

THE PEACE WE NEED.

Epheslans ll. 14.

FOR HE IS OUR PEACE WHO HATH MADE BOTH ONE, AND HATH BROKEN DOWN THE MIDDLE WALL OF PARTITION BETWEEN US.

WHAT can we do for our country? This question lies upon every heart. And the feeling will be, that no day could be more suitable for the consideration of it than the present. We are called, it is true, to mourning; summoned, in the fitting words of our President, "to humble ourselves before Almighty God," and to pray that our recent "bereavement may be sanctified to the nation." Of the greatness of this bereavement; of the character and services of our departed Chief Magistrate; of the inscrutable purpose of that Providence which permitted him to die, and that by an assassin's hand, at the very moment when the rebellion was tottering to its fall, and all his powers were absorbed in devising wise and generous plans for the early pacification of the country; of these and their kindred topics, I have already spoken to you. They have been the theme of three formal religious services in this house: and nothing has been omitted which could testify our mutual respect for the memory of the dead; and our profound sense of the solemnity with which God is addressing us in this awful and mysterious visitation. It will be quite in keeping with the spirit of these past observances, if we dedicate this day to the cause in which Mr. Lincoln sacrificed his life. From the hour Richmond fell, to the evening of his foul murder, the one thought which engrossed his mind, was, "How can we best secure a just and stable peace?" It appears to me that we can pay no better tribute to his memory, than by taking up this question, or its fair equivalent, "What can we do for our country?" and carefully weighing it in its bearing upon our personal duty.

The country will need the help of all its faithful children. We have been tried by four years of war. In no spirit of boasting, but with humble gratitude to God, we may claim, that the nation has borne this fiery ordeal better than could have been expected. Our government has withstood the shock of this mighty rebellion. Vast as has been the expenditure of men and means, our resources are not exhausted. We emerge from the sanguinary conflict, not defeated and dismembered, but still one people, under one government, and with an undivided country. For these priceless blessings let us offer our thanksgivings to God. But let it not be supposed that our work is done. We simply exchange one course of discipline for another. The return of peace will bring its trials not less certainly than the progress of the war.

With nations, as with individuals, success is a severe crucible to character. But this is a small part of the test to which we are to be subjected. The principles involved in this war, are those which lie at the very foundations of our government. Some of these have been decisively and, as we may hope, permanently settled. But others which have been evoked in the course of the contest, are still in controversy among the ablest and most patriotic friends of the Union. Still further, every great civil war, our own among them, gives birth to numerous questions among the most intricate upon which any government can be called to pass—questions of justice and mercy, of amnesty and indemnity, of reconstruction, of confiscation, of local military rule, and the like; in our case, multiplied and complicated by the unique and delicate relations of the Federal and State charters.

It is still more to our present purpose, to advert to the desolations caused by the war: the immense regions devastated; the breaking up of churches, and schools, and courts of justice; and the unavoidable demoralization incident to such a contest. Then there are the perils inseparable from the disbanding of large armies. There are questions concerning asylums and hospitals for the thousands of brave men who have suffered in defence of the country. There are the many difficult problems growing out of the abolition of slavery. And above all, there are the sorrows and the passions of the war; its bereavements, its wrongs, its estrangements, its implacable animosities.

All these things are before us. They may suffice (without enlarging the details,) to show something of the greatness and difficulty of the task devolved upon us. I do not say that the prospect should intimidate or discourage us. I do not feel this. He who has been with us in six troubles, in seven will not forsake us. But we must not shut our eyes to the realities of our condition. We are not to indulge the pleasant conceit that because, through God's blessing, the rebellion is subdued and the land purged of the taint of slavery, our trials are at an end and our work finished. Let us, rather, look at things as they are. Let us without fear and without passion survey the new field which is opened to us, and gird ourselves for its high demands.

A lofty mission it is that invites our efforts. To heal our country's wounds; to repair its desolations; to soothe its sorrows; to allay its enmities; to replace prejudice, discord, and confusion, with candor, respect, and kindness; and to resuscitate the various agencies, moral and material, which may cement the Union, and renew its prosperity;—this is the sublime task which invites the generous co-operation of all lovers of their country. Its difficulty is conceded. But there is a power—and only one—by which it can be accomplished. It is the power named in the text—THE RELIGION OF CHRIST: "For HE is our PEACE who hath made both one, and hath broken down the middle wall of partition between us." That solid and towering wall had for fifteen centuries separated the two races. The numerous assaults made upon it, were as abortive as javelins hurled against an armored vessel. It was invincible to force. Argument recoiled from it. Time, which changes all things, only strengthened its buttresses and enlarged its towers. Alike in prosperity and adversity, as a conqueror in Jerusalem and a captive in Babylon, as the lord of the Canaanite and the slave of the Roman, the Jew ceased not to despise the Gentile, as the Gentile, also, continued to hate the Jew. But there was One greater than Jew or Gentile who appeared among them, and died a malefactor's death. And, wonderful to relate, they who, agreeing in nothing else, struck hands to crucify Him, as they stood before His cross, felt their mutual enmity turn to love. The middle wall of partition between them fell down at His presence; the estrangements of centuries disappeared; and they mingled together as one fold under one Shepherd.

Here is hope for us. Such is the union *we* need, and such the means by which it can be effected. One may say this without disparaging the functions of the State. The rapid survey we have just taken of the condition of the country, may suffice to show the magnitude of the interests with which the State has to deal, and the difficulties it must grapple with in the settlement of our affairs. Into those matters it is not for the pulpit to intrude. Whenever our rulers need its advice in disposing of purely political questions, it is to be presumed they will ask it. Until then, it is not very apparent how anything is to be gained to the cause of public order or public virtue, by the pulpit's undertaking to dictate to the government what it shall do in respect to the punishment of treason, reconstruction, the extension of the suffrage, or any of the kindred topics now so much agitated. We may safely leave these questions where the Constitution and laws have lodged them. The disposition to bring them to the bar of the Church for adjudication, betrays, it appears to me, an unfortunate confusion of ideas concerning the respective spheres of the Church and the State, and must operate to the prejudice of both. For, on the one hand, it tends to unspiritualize the Church; and, on the other, it envenoms political disputes by infusing into them the proverbial rancor of theological controversy. There are ways in which the Church can help the State; and it may not innocently withhold its aid. Especially is it bound to come to its assistance in a great national struggle like that we have witnessed, and in adjusting the abstruse problems which grow out of it. But if it mistake the *means* and *methods* of relief, it may sadly mar the work it would promote.

The true way for the Church to help the State, is to confine itself to its own sphere, and do its own work. This is what its Founder did. There were grave political disputes pending at the period of His personal ministry. Every device was employed to induce him to take part in them. He steadfastly refused. The apostles, and the ministers who succeeded them, followed in his steps. And what was the result? With such persuasive and growing power did their teachings tell upon the State, that in a comparatively brief space of time the empire exchanged its Paganism for Christianity. Is it wise, or modest, or safe, to contemn our Saviour's example in an affair of such vital consequence to society, to the Church, to the whole world?

And why should the Church wish to arrogate the prerogatives of the civil magistrate? Its responsibilities are weighty enough already; so weighty that none of its friends need ask to have them augmented. Nor this alone. The mission confided to the Christianity of the country, is as beneficent as it is arduous. Such honor has God put upon it, that he calls it to do a work in the pacification of the country which the State *cannot* do. The grand object to be attained, that which underlies and pervades all the momentous issues now agitating the public mind, is to bring about a general and hearty reconciliation; to break down the wall of partition which has long divided the North and the South, and the barriers which may separate other portions of the people into hostile factions or parties; and make them all one, not in name merely, but in deed and in truth. To the government it belongs to re-organize our political system, and set in motion its complex mechanism. The formal union thus renewed, may be invigorated and cemented by the wholesome tendencies of commerce, of education, and of social intercourse. But these are only co-efficients. The true amalgam lies in that potential influence which availed to make Jew and Gentile "both one."

For no other agency can *reach the seat* of the malady to be cured. The ordinary contests of political parties are sufficiently virulent; but they are nothing to the case now before us. Here are sectional jealousies of many years standing, inflamed by the experiences of a protracted and bloody war. What with the exultation of victory and the chagrin of defeat, the losses and wrongs and desolations of the contest, and the vast changes it has wrought in the social and civil condition of the country and in the tone of the nation, it were puerile to suppose that the heart-burnings and resentments of such a period can be healed by any earthly specific. Fear or favor may secure obedience to law and outward tranquillity. But these may consort with implacable enmities. The advantage of Christianity is, that it lays the axe at the root of the evil. It goes down into the depths of the inner consciousness. It aims to "make the tree good;" to cast its living branch into the bitter fountain; content, when this is done, to leave the fruit and the streams to themselves.

Other reformers have recognized the importance of this, and have essayed to accomplish it. But they have uniformly failed, and for a common reason. There is but one Power in the universe strong enough to cope with the human heart; and they could not command it. Christianity does command it. The Gospel of Christ is God's appointed instrumentality for subduing and re-moulding human nature. In His hands, we are as clay in the hands of the potter. Whatever the antipathies and hatreds of this war, we need not distrust His power to remove them. Grace has wrought marvels even greater than this. We have seen it in the case of the Jews and Gentiles. It is going forward at this moment in Africa, in New Zealand, in Feejee; where men who but yesterday were cannibals, are to-day sitting at the feet of Jesus, clothed, and in their right mind. Nay, we have the evidence of it much nearer home. For who that has had his own enmity to God turned into love, can doubt as to the efficacy of the Gospel in allaying the worst animosities and healing the most pitiless quarrels between man and man?

The question, "Can the North and the South ever become one again in affection?" is heard on every side. And the negative answer it receives, is natural enough to those who regard it only from an earthly point of view. But "is anything too hard for the LORD?" Hopeless as the task might be in any other aspect, it ceases to be hopeless the moment it is understood that we may commit it into His hands. To do this in good faith, is the paramount duty of the hour. It is more than a duty. It is a great privilege. Rarely has God given to the Christians of a land, an opportunity like that He now offers us. We use no unguarded language when we assert, that the Christians of our country have it their power, by God's blessing, to bring about that thorough pacification for which all hearts are yearning. For, helpless as they are in themselves, the treasure of the Gospel is committed to their keeping, and the Gospel is the wisdom of God and the power of God. It has proved itself the most potent influence concerned in the affairs of the world,—stronger than the worst passions of the heart; stronger than prison walls; stronger than armies; stronger than the might of hoary empires; stronger than the Arch-apostate and all his hosts. And it has but to be applied, to achieve an early mastery over the asperities and separations of this war.

"*To be applied!*" Here is the point that concerns us. On the abstract question of the omnipotent energy of the Gospel, we must all be agreed. But is *our* Christianity equal to this emergency? Can it take in the grandeur and beneficence of the work to which it is summoned? Can it rise above the turmoil of earth, and address itself to its work in the temper of its Master? Allow that the provocations to the exercise of an opposite temper are very great: that this rebellion was marked with a flagitious criminality; that it has been attended with appalling barbarities; that the wrongs and sorrows it has inflicted upon the North, are too deep and too recent not to be most keenly felt. Concede, as we must, all this: does it, nevertheless, annul the obligation which rests upon us, to heed the teachings of Christ, and tread in his steps? The Christianity that draws its inspiration from the world; that recruits itself, not from the word of life and the throne of grace, but from the fury which at such crises inflames the passions of the multitude; is unworthy of the name it bears, and faithless to its Lord. It is no lesson of Christianity, that we extenuate the guilt of such a rebellion, or attempt to shield its authors from merited punishment, or say or do aught that may embarrass the functions of the government. It is not at all (I repeat the observation) with these topics I am dealing. I speak of our duty as professing Christians; and of the mission of the Church. And I say, that it is not for Christian men and women to go to the world for their inspiration: to adopt the principles, to cherish the resentments, and to deal out the maledictions common to those who are swayed by mere natural impulses.

The dictate of this earth-born philosophy, is, "Beware how you show kindness to those who have by word or deed given the slightest countenance to this rebellion. No matter what their surroundings at the time, let none of them ever again approach you. Shut your doors upon them. Never speak to them. Treat them to the end as your enemies." This is nature. And if the Church is to be leavened and controlled by this spirit, the war, though terminated in form, must go on indefinitely. "When will this war end?" said a friend to one of the bravest and noblest of our Major-Generals, one whose name is never mentioned by men of any section or party but with respect and gratitude.* "*When the nation is brought to exercise a penitent and forgiving spirit.*" Well said, Christian soldier: we need not ask in what school *thou* hast been taught. Nor need we fear that in the end, all true disciples of Christ will approve of this spirit. Amidst the scenes of horror and sadness which have lately passed before us, it is not surprising that exasperated feeling should have driven even some

* General Anderson.

Christian men from their moorings. But they are tolerably certain to come back to their anchorage. No one who has had experience of God's mercy will maintain, except under some gust of passion, that the priest and the Levite were right in "passing by on the other side," and that the Samaritan should have done the same. Such an one may try to argue himself into the belief that (like Jonah) he "does well" to indulge a stern, unforgiving spirit. But grace will prevail over nature, and truth over sophistry. He cannot quite obliterate from his heart those divine lessons, "Ye have heard that it hath been said, Thou shalt love thy neighbor and hate thine enemy. But I say unto you, *Love your enemies; bless them that curse you; do good to them that hate you; and pray for them which despitefully use you and persecute you.*" These words, enforced by that most touching of all prayers, "*Father, forgive them; for they know not what they do!*" make it very hard for a Christian to harbor vindictive feelings even towards those who may have grossly wronged him. Conscience will keep up its latent protest. And love will wrestle with hate. And by and by mercy will triumph over wrath; and He who heareth in secret, will hear the relenting brother cry, "Lord, lay not this sin to their charge!" Whenever *this* spirit comes to pervade the Church, the land will soon be healed of its deadly wounds.

Do not understand me as intimating by these observations, that this office of conciliation lies exclusively at our door. The obligations imposed by our religion, rest upon all who bear the Christian name. If I refer to our own sins, it is because the recognized object of a day of humiliation is to consider our own sins, not those of our neighbors. If I dwell upon our own duties, it is for the obvious reason that they are our own. And it were of slight avail to set forth here the sins and duties of people who are a thousand miles away. Could I make my voice to be heard at the South, I should not stop with inculcating these lessons of kindness and forbearance which I am urging upon you. In a great contest like this, it is not for man to apportion among different classes, the criminality which may attach to each. But if (as you have been constantly taught from this pulpit) rebellion against lawful government be a sin, then the ministers and churches of the South have assumed a fearful responsibility in the part they have acted in this war. The imperative requisition Christianity lays upon them, is, that they repent of this great iniquity; and return without delay, and counsel others to return, to their allegiance. And assuredly it is for them, no less than for ourselves, to exercise charity towards their brethren: to seek to renew the bonds of Christian fellowship which have been so rudely sundered: and to leave nothing undone which may help to redress the grievous injuries inflicted through their agency both upon the country and upon the cause of Christ.

But our personal concern with this matter is nearer home. Enough that the whole land needs, and must have, the ameliorating influence of pure and undefiled religion; and that the necessity for it is becoming more apparent every day. We have reached an epoch when we cannot dispense with it. So radical are the changes in our condition, occasioned by the war, that we may justly regard ourselves as entering upon a new and pregnant cycle in our career. This is clearly the popular sentiment. It meets us in all our Journals. It is the favorite common-place of political orators. It is the burden of our social gatherings. It is a familiar topic with the pulpit. All eyes are bent towards the future; and all tongues (or nearly all) are depicting the career of unexampled triumph and splendor which awaits us. This is not surprising. The resources developed by the war, have caused as much astonishment among ourselves, as among other nations. And the feeling has sprung up, that a people endowed with such apparently inexhaustible means and capable of such achievements, may count upon attaining a renown which will pale the lustre of all other kingdoms. The indisputable fact in our condition, is, that the various elements of power pertaining to our lot, have been stimulated to an intense activity. The country is all alive. Alike in the realms of matter and of mind; in every sphere of thought and in every department of labor; in literature, science, and morals; in husbandry, mechanics, and commerce; no less than in politics and martial affairs; everything has acquired, or is acquiring, a momentum which cannot fail to work out vast results for good or for ill. Whether for good or for ill, is a question of profound moment; and one that is likely to depend largely upon the use to which we put our Christianity. It needs no Daniel or Isaiah to predict how far the golden visions of our enthusiasts will be realized, if with this sudden revival of all the secular agencies which shape the destinies of nations, we miss a revival of the spirit and practice of true religion. There is no other power strong enough to hallow and control these restless elements. And by so much as they are whetted into this unwonted vigor, by thus much do they require to be attempered and guided by the sacred energy of the Gospel.

The exigency which demands this saving influence

is upon us now. The transition from war to peace involves a severe trial of national character. In our case the delicacy and hazards of the change, are augmented by the nature of the contest in which we have been engaged, and by the gigantic size of our armies. Here are a half million of men (North and South) to be disbanded. The principles and habits they have acquired in the garrison and the camp, are to be exchanged for the sober pursuits of trade and agriculture. The excitement which has formed so large a part of the daily aliment of the country for four years, is to be withdrawn. The energies of the nation are to be trained into new channels, and directed to objects as foreign as possible from marches and battles, and defeats and victories. Such a revolution will tax the virtue of our people as severely as that through which they passed in so abruptly exchanging the plough and the anvil for the sword and the musket. We need not distrust the issue. But every one must see that the experiment will put a fresh strain upon our social and political system; and that all the resources our Christianity can command, will be required to conduct it to a successful issue. This is the only lever by which the country can be let down gently and safely from a state of war to a state of peace.

This, however, is but the first step. If we would

guard against disaster in the new career upon which we are entering, the nation at large (as just intimated) must be more thoroughly impregnated with the influence of genuine religion. To this benign influence we may look to work some amelioration in our politics. Long before the war, the tendency to deterioration in this quarter had become too glaring to be denied. Good men of all parties united in reprobating the acrimony, the duplicity, and the venality, which were carried into our elections; as they also deplored the prevailing and criminal indifference to politics among so large a portion of the best citizens of the Union. We have paid the penalty of these grave delinquencies. Let not the lesson be lost upon us. The remedy is as obvious as it is practicable. It lies not with the pulpit. When the pulpit meddles with party politics, it becomes an engine of mischief. But it may and must enforce upon the people the duty of carrying into their politics the truthfulness, the integrity, and the charity, to which they are bound in every other sphere. This is the reform we need. There is intelligence, and honor, and Christian rectitude enough in the country to effect it. And piety and patriotism alike demand that no effort shall be spared for accomplishing it.

If I forbear to dwell upon the necessity of a

revived Christianity as the only adequate counteractive to the alarming growth of dishonesty throughout the land, it is simply because I have on other occasions said all that I cared to say to you on this subject.

But there are two phenomena in our condition too vitally connected with the subject before us, to be passed over in silence. One of these, is the colonizing of the immense regions lying between the Mississippi river and the Pacific ocean. The volume of emigration now pouring itself into those regions, is without precedent. Not only are most of the existing Territories preparing to put on the habiliments of States, but still other States formed out of that broad area will soon be knocking at our door for admission into the Union. There is room enough there for as many separate commonwealths as were included in the original confederation. Who would have it otherwise? Let them come and welcome—laden with their corn and wine and oil, and glittering in raiment of gold and silver, outvying the visions of Oriental fable. But to make them doubly welcome; to insure their coming as an element of strength and not of weakness to the Republic; we must see to it that these endless trains winding across our Western prairies, take the Bible with them; that the foundations of these new States be laid, not upon slavery, not upon abstract and unsanctified theories of liberty, not upon mere prowess and enterprise, but, in the faith and fear of God, upon the immutable principles of his word. We must see to it, that the CHURCH and the SCHOOL pitch their tents beside every encampment, and take possession of every village and hamlet. And we must never lose sight of the fact, that if these distant communities are to be clasped indissolubly to the older States, we must not trust implicitly to charters and rail-roads, but superadd to these the sacred bonds which "HE who is our PEACE" will throw around them.

The other topic referred to is the anomalous condition of the South. We cannot mistake in assuming that the rebellion has shattered, where it has not completely disorganized, both the educational and the ecclesiastical systems in the Southern and Border States. To repair these ruins; to rebuild churches and school-houses; to renew the ordinances of the Sanctuary; to disseminate the Scriptures; and, generally, to sustain and diffuse the healthful influence of the Gospel of Christ throughout those desolated regions:—here is a mission to be undertaken by the Church, the importance of which cannot be exaggerated. But this is only a part of the truth. Here are four millions of emancipated slaves to be cared for. Whatever diversity of sentiment may have existed in respect to slavery, all will agree as to the gravity of the problems springing out of its abrogation. Most of these fall within the purview of the civil authority. Our concern as Christians with the subject, is twofold. In some form, this great mass of ignorant people must be brought under the influence of a thorough religious training. This is indispensable to themselves, and not less so to the white population. Without it, there can be neither tranquillity nor safety for either race. It pertains exclusively to the Christianity of the country, to devise the proper system or systems for effecting this object. When I say "the Christianity of the country," I do not mean that the Churches of the Union are to do this thing in their aggregate capacity, or that they are all to take a direct part in it. I simply mean that it is a Christian work, and Christians must do it,—trusting, however, that in the spirit of Him who "makes both one," and who has now broken down one of the great "walls of partition" between us, the day may not be distant when the Churches of the South and the Churches of the North shall be found shoulder to shoulder and heart to heart in carrying it forward.

Our further concern with the matter lies here.

The inherent difficulty of many of the political questions concerning the African race, soon to be officially passed upon, is admitted. Everything, then, will depend, under God, upon the spirit in which these questions are approached. What the emergency demands on the part of the federal government, and especially on the part of the Southern people, their legislatures, courts, and municipal authorities, is, preëminently, a spirit of wisdom, of justice, and of humanity. There is an urgent necessity that the whole social structure, South and North, be imbued with this temper; that so, the great experiment may proceed upon righteous principles, and result well for both the American and the African, and for our common country. This temper can emanate from only a single source—even from "HIM who is our PEACE." That Divine faith of which He is equally the spring and object, and the burden of which is, "peace on earth, good-will toward men," must be brought to bear in the fulness of its love and mercy, upon the magistracy of the land, and upon our whole people. Let us hope that under its heavenly guidance, the two races may, by God's blessing, thread this perilous labyrinth, and come forth at length into a "wealthy place."

These are merely specific illustrations of the general truth, that *the pervading presence and power of the Gospel of Christ, is the grand necessity of our country.* In every quarter it needs instruction and consolation. It needs to be guarded against despondency and against presumption. It needs to be purged of the pride and vainglory which have defaced its strength and splendor. It needs to be at peace with God; that so the peace to be established within its borders, may be just and pure and lasting. It needs to be taught that without the Divine blessing, the wisdom of our statesmen, the courage of our armies, the skill and industry of our people, and our opulent resources of every kind, will prove but as chaff before the fire. It needs to have all classes and conditions of our population coming together once more in a spirit of mutual forbearance and amity, and combining their efforts to retrieve the ruins of the war and renew our former prosperity. These wants are universal and pressing. Wise legislation, and the proverbial energy of our people, may do something toward supplying them. But they are not to be compassed by any earth-born sagacity. They make their appeal to the Church of God; to those who having been imbued with the spirit of the Great PHYSICIAN and PEACE-MAKER, can invoke His Omnipotent grace and His unerring wisdom, to provide for our necessities, and do for us "exceeding abundantly above all that we ask or think."

This is the proper office of the Church. By the merciful provision of her Divine Head, she is set to instruct the world; to enlighten its ignorance, to rectify its false judgments, to set before it the teachings of God's word, to assist it in understanding the lessons of his Providence. Her mission, further, is to keep alive in the world a sense of His supremacy; to foster in men's minds a feeling of their dependence; to check the ebullitions of passion; to repress unholy tempers; to strengthen the arm of justice; to vindicate the cause of truth and righteousness against all violence, treachery, and calumny; and to nourish, as well in nations as in individuals, the habit of viewing God in everything, and everything in God.

Such being the nature and design of the Church, it is of the last importance, that she should not now mistake her calling, nor decline the service to which the course of events so clearly calls her. We are all looking with a natural solicitude to our government,—as we have been for the past four years, to our fleets and armies. But if the Scriptures teach any lesson adapted to our circumstances, it is, that the future of the country depends much more upon the CHURCH than upon all human agencies put together. There is no interest of earth so dear to God as his Church. It is the only organization he has preserved from the beginning. He has founded nations and dynasties without number, and extinguished them. We read history blindfolded if we do not see, that empires and governments are of slight account with him, except in their relations to that immortal kingdom, which, like the stone cut out of the mountain, is to break in pieces and destroy all other kingdoms. His eye is upon the righteous of a land. They it is who "have power" with him. Their fidelity to God is the most vital element of a nation's prosperity. And their general defection is always to be marked as one of the surest sources of a nation's overthrow.

These principles, familiar to every student of the Bible, should not be lost sight of now. Our Christianity is on trial. The responsibility devolved upon it by this solemn juncture in our affairs, is great beyond description. Holding, as it does, the only balm that can soothe the country's wounds, and the only cordial for its sorrows, it has but to exert its healing powers, and all will be well. And then, when the day of reckoning comes, it shall have no cause to complain of the penury of its reward.

There are those who will deride this strain of remark as betraying a needless anxiety about our future: who feel that having triumphed over this rebellion, we can afford to smile at all other difficulties. And undoubtedly the goodness of God, in bringing us successfully through the war, should make us hopeful as to His favor hereafter. We may well feel encouraged as to the final issue of these extraordinary scenes; but *only* as we trust in "HIM who is our PEACE." Had our CHRISTIANITY as a nation been what it should have been, the rebellion could not have happened; and we had been spared these four years' of bloodshed and sorrow. We have committed the fatal mistake of permitting our material and political, to outstrip very far our spiritual, growth. To repeat the error after this terrible rebuke, will be to invite fresh judgments. For what are the most powerful nations without God's protection, when a miserable caitiff may in an instant of time plunge twenty millions of people into mourning? If we would insure for ourselves a prosperous future, we must become a more thoroughly *religious* people. Standing as in the shadow of that great sorrow which chills the joy of returning peace, let us resolve to render our country the noblest service she can receive from any of her children, by doing everything in our power to diffuse far and wide the influence of a pure Christianity. Let us do what we can to retrieve the moral wastes of the war; to establish Churches; to circulate the Scriptures; to sustain evangelical Missions. While unfeignedly thankful for the issue of the late contest, let us testify our grateful appreciation of peace, by allowing the passions of war to die with the war.

Let the love of Christ constrain us to repress in ourselves, and discountenance in others, "all bitterness, and wrath, and anger, and clamor, and evil speaking, and all malice." Let us carry into every sphere of life the forbearance and the charity which we daily need and daily experience at the hands of our Heavenly Father. Let us invoke the special blessing of God upon our President, who, acceding to that high dignity under circumstances of such deep solemnity, has already shown himself so worthy of the cordial respect and confidence of the country. Let us cease not to intercede with God for him, and for all our rulers; that He may shield them from violence, sustain them under their burdens, and endue them with wisdom, patience, firmness, and humanity in the discharge of their responsible duties. Let us further commend to His loving care the mourners all over the land; and plead with Him so to sanctify our national bereavement, and all the afflictions of the war, that the nation may come out of this furnace purified as gold that has been tried in the fire. Thus shall we find the promised Messiah to be our PEACE: every wall of partition will be broken down; and our restored civil UNION will but typify that deeper, holier union which has made us "ALL ONE IN CHRIST JESUS."

Lightning Source UK Ltd.
Milton Keynes UK
UKHW021039110119
335297UK00012B/1748/P

9 780483 034174